Marquette University

Student Prayer Book

Office of the President

Dear Marquette Student,

One of our privileges as believers is to pray directly to God. Each of our religious traditions offers prayers that assist us in our approach to the Almighty. Since all of us occasionally trip over our words to God, it is useful to have some prayers that express our deep religious convictions and also stimulate us to formulate our own words to God.

Just as I want you to develop intellectually, socially and affectively during your years at Marquette, I also want you to grow spiritually. College is a time of tremendous growth, and it is important that your spirituality continue to deepen. This book is meant to serve as a source of power for you.

The prayers contained in this book have been recommended by a variety of students, faculty, and staff. Most of these prayers stem from the Judeo-Christian tradition, but many of them can also be comfortably used by people of other faiths.

May the Marquette University Student Prayer Book help you to pray regularly and to grow in your faith each year you are at Marquette.

Prayerfully,

Albert J. DiUlio, S.J.
President

General Contents

Preface

This collection has a threefold purpose. First, it presents prayers, poems, and hymns that express deep human sentiments to our Lord and God. Many of these have been used by generations of Catholics to praise and thank God. Second, the book offers a brief introduction to the Jesuit heritage. Although Marquette could not function without the dedication of hundreds of faculty, staff, and administrators who are committed to the Jesuit tradition, the tradition itself cannot thrive unless students are aware of at least some important Jesuits and their achievements, as well as the names of Jesuit colleges and universities in the United States. Third, the illustrations are intended to assist a person's imagination. God invites us to pray in words that we choose. Because we do not often hear other people praying intimately, most of us find it easier at first to rely on the written prayers of others. These written prayers can be the starting point for our own conversation with God.

A complete list of acknowledgments is given at the end of the book. However, I wish to thank certain people in a special way. Father John Patrick Donnelly wrote all of the historical material on Saint Ignatius, the Jesuits, and individual saints and holy people. Katie Oberhauser created the attractive drawings, and Casey Beaumier, in addition to writing some of the prayers, carefully reviewed the text and prepared it for printing.

> John J. Piderit, S.J.
> Editor

Specific Contents

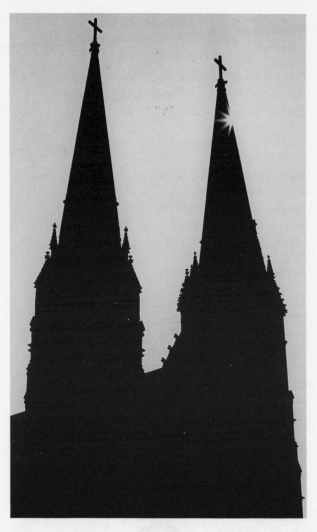

Worship at Marquette

The Church of the Gesu
by *Michael J. Burns*

The Church of the Gesu, located in the middle of the Marquette University campus, is one of the most impressive campus churches of the world. The Gesu was constructed under the direction of Herman Esser, a partner in the noted architectural firm of H.C. Koch and Company, and was dedicated December 16, 1894. Although much of the Gesu brings to mind English Gothic (the sanctuary is similar to the arcade of Litchfield Cathedral, and the narthex is clearly modeled after several of the college churches at Oxford), the prevailing design is the Rayonnant style, which was popular in France during the thirteenth and fourteenth centuries.

The exterior of the building is Bedford stone. The extreme exterior length from the north entrance to the southern wall is 199 feet. The extreme exterior width, including the transepts, is 135 feet. The Gesu is seventy feet high at the crossing. The west tower is 250 feet high and the east is 215 feet. The Gesu has space for more than 1,000 worshippers and the undercroft can hold 500.

There are twelve windows in the nave, and they depict the birth, life and death of Christ. The thirty-five windows of the clerestory represent important figures of the people of God: the Patriarchs and the Prophets of Israel, Christ, Mary and Joseph, Saints Anne, Andrew, Patrick, Gall, Thomas Aquinas, Ignatius Loyola, and John Francis Regis, among others. The windows were made at the Royal Bavarian Institute for Stained Glass in Munich, Germany, under supervision of the noted German artist Franz Xavier Zettler.

The main entrance, constructed from funds given in memory of Eugene Lonstorf, a member of the Marquette College Class of 1896 who died before graduation, was completed in 1901. The undercroft, dedicated to Saint Rose of Lima, was completed in 1910.

The altars in the Gesu, which date from 1927, were gifts of Mrs. Harriet L. Cramer, a generous benefactor of Marquette University.

Saint Joan of Arc

Saint Joan of Arc, born at Domremy in Lorraine in 1412, was an ordinary medieval peasant girl until she started to hear voices which urged her to free France from the English invaders during the Hundred Years' War. For five years she kept these secret, but in 1429 she stole away from home and went to Charles VII. The King had her examined by theologians before agreeing to follow her advice. For a peasant girl to command the royal army was almost unthinkable! Yet the King agreed. He had little to lose since he had already lost the richest parts of France. Joan's army lifted the siege of Orleans in a brilliant campaign, then again defeated an English army, thereby opening the way for Charles' coronation at Reims in 1429. That was the turning point away from ninety-two years of French defeats.

Joan fought another battle against the Burgundians in 1420 and was captured. They sold her to their English allies. The English could not be content merely to execute their prime enemy; they had to discredit her first. If her voices were from God, then the English cause in the war was against God.

Joan was put on trial as a heretic at Rouen and interrogated for three months in 1431. She was tricked into admission of guilt; this allowed the judge to sentence her as a relapsed heretic. He turned her over to the secular authorities who burned her at the stake on May 30 (now her feast day). As the flames rose, she protested her innocence.

A Church court rehabilitated Joan in 1456, and she was canonized in 1920. The writers of many novels and plays, for instance, George Bernard Shaw, have used her life and death to push their own agendas.

Saint Joan of Arc Chapel

The Saint Joan of Arc Chapel is more than five centuries old. It was originally from a little French village, Chasse, and was known as the Chapelle de St. Martin de Sayssuel. After the French Revolution, the Chapel fell into ruin where it was left until after the First World War. It was then restored by an architect named Jacques Couelle.

In 1926 Gertrude Hill Gavin, the daughter of James J. Hill, the American railroad magnate, acquired the Chapel, and it was transferred to her fifty-acre estate on Long Island. The reconstruction plans were developed by one of America's leading architects, John Russell Pope, who also planned the National Gallery in Washington, D.C.

In 1962, the Gavin estate passed into the possession of Mr. and Mrs. Marc B. Rojtman. In 1964 the Rojtmans presented the Chapel to Marquette and had it

dismantled and sent to the campus for reassembly.
The dismantling on Long Island began in June 1964
and took nine months to complete. A fleet of trucks,
each vehicle carrying forty thousand pounds, brought
the Chapel stones to Milwaukee, where reconstruction
began in July 1965. The Chapel was dedicated to St.
Joan of Arc on May 26, 1966.

The Chapel of the Holy Family

Another special place of prayer and worship at
Marquette is the Chapel of the Holy Family, located in
the Alumni Memorial Union adjacent to the Office of
Campus Ministry.

This chapel was completed in the fall of 1990, and it
can seat 200 people.

Saint Ignatius Loyola
and Jesuit History

Saint Ignatius Loyola

Ignatius of Loyola (1491-1556) was born in
northern Spain of a noble Basque family in the castle
called Loyola. The year after his birth Ferdinand
and Isabella conquered Granada, the last Moorish
stronghold in Spain, and sent Columbus in search of
China. A decade later two of Loyola's brothers
fought with the Spanish armies that conquered
Naples, another helped crush a revolt in Granada,
and a fourth sailed for America. Loyola's youth was
spent mainly as a page at two noble courts, and
during his twenties he served as a courtier and heard
about how an obscure German friar, Martin Luther,
was questioning the basis of medieval Christianity.

Loyola was not trained as a professional soldier,
but a courtier was expected to take up his sword in
an emergency. This Loyola did when the French
invaded northern Spain in 1521. Loyola was
wounded trying to defend the city of Pamplona;
impressed by his valor, his French captors sent him
back to Loyola Castle to recover. There he began
reading the lives of Christ and the saints when no
novels of chivalry could be found. Gradually he
came to realize that daydreams about imitating the
saints in serving God gave more inward relish than
daydreams of knightly deeds.

He determined to go as a pilgrim to Jerusalem
and live there. He headed for the port of Barcelona,

but on the way he paused for a few days in the small town of Manresa to write some spiritual notes. The stop dragged on for ten months as he meditated on Christ's life. His prayer gradually deepened into mystical experiences. The notes he took down at Manresa became the nucleus of his great book *The Spiritual Exercises*, which allow others to share his insights and experiences. Over the next twenty years Loyola added to these notes and directed various followers through the Exercises, a spiritual retreat of thirty days.

The Spiritual Exercises break into four "weeks": the first deals with the purpose of life, the second with Christ's public life, the third with his passion and death, and the fourth with his resurrection. The first printed edition of *The Spiritual Exercises* appeared at Rome in 1548. Since then this little book, devoid of literary grace but potent in spiritual teaching, has enjoyed more than 5,000 editions in dozens of languages.

Traveling through Barcelona, Rome, and Venice, Loyola reached Jerusalem in mid 1523, but Church authorities insisted he return to Europe. He then decided that if he were to help others find Christ, he needed an education. At age thirty-three, surrounded by adolescent boys, he spent two years at a grammar school in Barcelona so he could master enough Latin to enroll in a university. He then attended the Universities of Alcala and Salamanca, but in both places his efforts to bring others to Christ aroused suspicion from the Inquisition and other authorities. His efforts also cut into his study time. Loyola determined to go the University of Paris, where he would get a more systematic training.

At Paris, Loyola, like students down the centuries, had no money, and so he begged for his living from wealthy merchants. Two years after his arrival he was assigned new quarters, where his roommates were Blessed Peter Favre and Saint Francis Xavier. Gradually he won them over to his spiritual ideals; in time he attracted four others. The seven companions were international from the beginning: two Basques, three from Castile, one from Portugal and one from Savoy. In 1534 these seven men pronounced vows of poverty and chastity and a promise to work for souls in Palestine when they finished their studies. If they could not go to Palestine, they would put themselves at the Pope's service.

Loyola returned to Spain to settle his affairs and recover his health, then moved on to Venice to await his companions (plus several new recruits) and sail for Palestine. But a war between Venice and the Muslim Turks in 1537 prevented their departure.

They put themselves at Pope Paul III's service, who used them as preachers and teachers. The companions decided they would need more structure if they were to serve God efficiently. They discussed ways of organizing their work and life together; Loyola drew up a document reflecting their discussions and presented it to Pope Paul III, who gave his oral approval to the new religious order in 1540. His companions elected Loyola its first superior general. For the rest of his life Loyola worked on the 1540 draft until he finished the long and elaborate Jesuit Constitutions, which were approved two years after his death.

The new order grew very rapidly, adding a thousand members before Loyola's death. Unlike earlier orders such as the Benedictines, Franciscans and Dominicans, the Jesuits did not sing in choir but only read privately the Divine Office traditionally said by priests. This allowed them to devote more time to their ministries, which soon branched out. Francis Xavier became the great missionary to the Orient. Reluctantly, the Jesuits opened schools and colleges, but education gradually became their main work. Several Jesuits served as nuncios, or papal ambassadors. Others preached, did parish work, and gave the Spiritual Exercises. Two of Loyola's first companions from Paris served as chaplains in the forces of Emperor Charles V, one in Germany, the other in Africa.

For his last fifteen years Loyola was the mystic and administrator; he alternated his time between prayer and paper work—almost 7000 of his letters from these years survive. But also he found time for several personal ministries. He organized noble women to rescue young girls from prostitution, setting up a half-way house to rehabilitate them. He even opened a convent for ex-prostitutes. He set up a home for poor abandoned girls and refinanced a similar home for boys. At the instance of his followers, he wrote an autobiography of his early life, but burned most of his private spiritual notes shortly before his death on July 31, 1556. He was canonized in 1622.

The Jesuits

The Jesuits, or the Society of Jesus, to use the official title, grew out of six student companions gathered by Ignatius of Loyola at the University of Paris in the 1530s. When their original project of going as missionaries to Palestine was blocked by war, they put themselves at the service of Pope Paul III. Gradually they came to see the need for rules and structures if their work and union in serving God were to continue and increase. They formed a religious order, elected Loyola as their superior general, and obtained papal approval in 1540. Orders of monks such as the Benedictines dedicated almost all their effort to prayer; the medieval orders of friars such as the Dominicans and Franciscans tried to mix ministry toward others with prayer; the Jesuits tilted the balance strongly in favor of helping others, striving to find God precisely in an active ministry.

The Catholic Church was facing the crisis of the Protestant Reformation when the Jesuits were founded. By seeking to break away from Rome, the Protestants encouraged efforts at reform within Catholicism. The Council of Trent clarified Catholic doctrine, the popes largely turned from political power games and art patronage to religious revival, new religious orders sprung up—Capuchins, Ursulines, and Oratorians, besides the Jesuits.

Initial Jesuit growth was slow in northern Europe but rapid in Spain and most rapid in Portugal and Sicily, where Islam was the threat, not Martin Luther. By 1565 there were 3500 Jesuits, by 1626 the Jesuits probably reached the zenith of their influence and counted 15,544 members. Their growth was slower during the next century, largely because they lacked the money to train candidates.

The first Jesuits made their mark as preachers, convent reformers, and missionaries, but in 1548 the Jesuits opened their first college intended for lay students at Messina in Sicily. It was an instant success, and petitions for more Jesuits colleges flowed into Rome from most of the cities of Catholic Europe. Quickly, education became the main Jesuit ministry. By 1579 the Jesuits were operating 144 colleges (most admitted students between twelve and twenty) in Europe, Asia, and Latin America. By 1749 the Jesuits were staffing 669 colleges and 235 seminaries world-wide. The Jesuit system of education, building on the curriculum devised by Renaissance humanists, was codified in the *Ratio Studiorum* of 1599. This approach controlled Jesuit education until the late nineteenth century, when American Jesuit universities began to make adjustments to the conditions in the United States. Marquette University was a pioneer in educating women, first in nursing and education, then in other disciplines.

With education went writing books—textbooks, catechisms, scholarly works in theology and philosophy, answers to Protestant polemics, scripture studies, plays written for production at Jesuit colleges, descriptions of the peoples and parts of the world visited by Jesuit missionaries. The Jesuits introduced China to Western science and philosophy. Among the Jesuit writers noted elsewhere in this prayer book are Robert Bellarmine, Peter Canisius, Edmund Campion, and Gerard Manley Hopkins.

Missionary work has always been among the most prized of Jesuit ministries, from Francis Xavier to the present. In Loyola's lifetime, missions were opened in Africa, India, Malaysia, Indonesia, and Japan. Ten years later there were Jesuit missionaries working in North and South America. Jesuits often had to work underground in countries whose rulers persecuted Catholics, and many suffered martyrdom— as did Edmund Campion, Paul Miki and Miguel Pro, who are treated elsewhere in this prayer book. Today, roughly 8,000 of the world's 24,000 Jesuits work in Third World countries.

The Jesuits have made many enemies for many different reasons during their long history. In the mid-eighteenth century they were hated by the philosophes, many of them deists, for their religious faith. The Jesuits were distrusted by the Enlightened Despots because they opposed growing state control of religion and supported the pope. The kings of Portugal, France, Spain and Naples, urged on by advisors who were disciples of the philosophes, first drove the Jesuits from their own lands, then forced the pope to suppress the Order around the world in 1773. Thanks to a technicality in the Brief of Suppression and the benevolence of Catherine the Great, the Jesuits survived in Russia.

Because of the Suppression, the Jesuits played only a small role in the first decades of the American Catholic Church, but a former Jesuit, John Carroll was the first American bishop. Other former Jesuits, notably Pierre de la Clorivière, played crucial roles in the establishment of congregations of teaching nuns, who were to be the backbone of American Catholic education in the era 1850-1950.

After the era of the French Revolution and Napoleon, there was a reaction to the ideas of the Enlightenment and a religious revival. Pope Pius VII restored the Jesuits worldwide in 1814. By 1830 there were 2,137 Jesuits, by 1900 there were 15,073. The high point came in mid-1960s with 36,000 Jesuits. In the last quarter century membership in almost all religious orders has declined, the Jesuits included.

Still, the Jesuits remain the largest male religious order. While their numbers have decreased sharply in Western Europe and considerably in the United States, their numbers in Third World countries, especially Africa and India, and in Eastern Europe are growing. The Jesuits continue to operate a unique network of schools around the world, most notably in the United States, where there are twenty

Jesuit universities, almost all in large cities and eight Jesuit colleges. There are also Jesuit universities in such cities as Rome, Madrid, Beirut, Manila, Tokyo and Seoul. Jesuit periodicals appear in most of the world's major languages, and some 500 Jesuits work in the communications media, mainly in the Third World. At the latest count 4,485 Jesuits belonged to the ten American Provinces. Several hundred other American Jesuits were members of provinces in missionary countries.

Jesuit Facts – 1993

—23,771 Jesuits serve worldwide. 16,699 priests, 2,884 brothers, and 4,188 scholastics.

—There are 1,007 novices.

—Jesuits serve in 112 nations.

—One-fifth of the world's Jesuits are assigned to foreign missions; 500 United States Jesuits serve abroad.

—Jesuits sponsor 45 high schools and 28 colleges and universities in the United States.

—Over 750 Jesuits serve in the ministries of higher education in the United States.

—400 Jesuit priests and brothers staff the 115 Jesuit parishes in the United States.

—Over 200 Jesuits serve in 29 retreat houses and spiritual centers in the United States.

U.S. Jesuit Colleges and Universities

Boston College	Boston, MA
Canisius College	Buffalo, NY
College of the Holy Cross	Worcester, MA
Creighton University	Omaha, NE
Fairfield University	Fairfield, CT
Fordham University	New York City, NY
Georgetown University	Washington, D.C.
Gonzaga University	Spokane, WA
John Carroll University	Cleveland, OH
Le Moyne College	Syracuse, NY
Loyola College in Maryland	Baltimore, MD
Loyola-Marymount Univ.	Los Angeles, CA
Loyola University, Chicago	Chicago, IL
Loyola Univ., New Orleans	New Orleans, LA
Marquette University	Milwaukee, WI
Regis University	Denver, CO
Rockhurst College	Kansas City, MO
Saint Joseph's University	Philadelphia, PA
Saint Louis University	St. Louis, MO
Saint Peter's College	Jersey City, NJ
Santa Clara University	Santa Clara, CA
Seattle University	Seattle, WA
Spring Hill College	Mobile, AL
University of Detroit Mercy	Detroit, MI
University of San Francisco	San Francisco, CA
University of Scranton	Scranton, PA
Wheeling Jesuit College	Wheeling, WV
Xavier University	Cincinnati, OH

Some
Noteworthy Jesuits

Jacques Marquette and Marquette University

Jacques Marquette, S.J., was a renowned Jesuit missionary and explorer. Father Marquette and Louis Joliet, along with five companions, were the first Europeans to explore the Mississippi River.

Father Marquette was born June 1, 1637 in Laon, France. He entered the Society of Jesus at the age of seventeen. After his ordination, he traveled to Quebec, introducing Christianity to Native Americans. He moved from tribe to tribe by following rivers.

In the course of his two-year journey exploring the Mississippi River, he recorded information regarding the topography and animal life in the Midwest.

On May 18, 1675, Father Marquette died at the age of thirty-seven near the present-day city of Ludington, Michigan.

Father Marquette's life testifies to faith, service, and discovery, a rich legacy and a continual challenge to Marquette University.

The origins of Marquette University date from 1848 when the Most Reverend John Martin Henni, first bishop of Milwaukee, obtained money to establish a Jesuit college. In 1855 Jesuits agreed to staff St. Gall's Parish, but they lacked personnel for a college.

The Wisconsin Legislature eventually granted a charter for Marquette College in 1864, and in 1881 seven Jesuits opened the college in September. By the end of that year, 77 students were enrolled. The first graduation was held in 1887 with five students receiving Bachelor of Arts degrees.

Saint Robert Bellarmine

Saint Robert Bellarmine (1542-1621), an Italian, entered the Jesuits in 1560. He quickly showed great talent in languages, philosophy, and theology. After six years teaching at Louvain, Belgium, he became professor of controversial theology at Rome in 1576. He published dozens of books, including a famous catechism. In 1599 he was named a cardinal and worked closely with a number of popes. His last twenty years were devoted to administration and writing.

Saint Paul Miki

Saint Paul Miki (1564-1597) was born in Japan. Francis Xavier brought Christianity to Japan in 1549, where its rapid growth (there were 200,000 Christians by 1590) alarmed Japanese rulers and forced the church underground. Paul Miki's family converted when he was still a boy. He entered the Jesuits in 1586; just before his ordination to the priesthood, he was arrested with two other Japanese Jesuits. The three Jesuits were crucified with six Franciscan friars and fifteen other Japanese.

Matteo Ricci

Matteo Ricci (1550-1610) pioneered Jesuit efforts to christianize China. He studied science and mathematics at Rome, theology in India, and Chinese at Macao. The Jesuit strategy for China was to use western science to win the respect and support of Chinese intellectuals and gain the Emperor's assent to Christian preaching. Speaking and writing Chinese and wearing mandarin robes, Ricci established a Jesuit residence at Beijing in 1601 where for 150 years Jesuit scientists and scholars secured imperial favor and fostered interchange between eastern and western intellectuals.

Robert de Nobili

Robert de Nobili's career (1577-1656) parallels that of Matteo Ricci, a Jesuit working in China. He entered the Jesuits in 1596 and sailed for India after eight years of study. Before Nobili, Indian Christians were westernized and lived under Portuguese protection. Nobili felt that Indian Christianity should retain as much Indian culture and customs as were compatible with the faith. He learned Tamil and Sanskrit and studied ancient Indian religion. In 1623 Gregory XV approved his approach, and he converted 4,000 Indians, many of them Brahmins, the elite who earlier had scorned Christianity.

Blessed Miguel Pro

Blessed Miguel Pro (1891-1927), who was born and raised in Mexico, entered the Jesuits in 1911, but a bitterly anti-Catholic regime forced Jesuit seminarians to flee to California in 1914. After studies in California, Spain, and Belgium, Pro returned home one month before the government closed every church in Mexico. Soldiers hunted down priests, who distributed the sacraments in secret. Pro was arrested and executed. His last cry as he faced the firing squad was, "Long live Christ the King."

Saint Peter Claver

Saint Peter Claver (1580-1654) attended the Jesuit college at Barcelona and entered the Jesuits in 1602. Eight years later he was assigned to Cartagena, Colombia, then the world's greatest slave market. Peter devoted his life to meeting slave ships. The voyage from Africa usually killed a third of the Africans; survivors were shattered in body and spirit. Peter brought them food, compassion and Christian faith. In forty-four years he baptized 300,000 Africans.

Saint Aloysius Gonzaga

Saint Aloysius Gonzaga (1568-1591) was the heir
to an illustrious Italian noble family and spent his
youth as a page at the Spanish court. But courtly
pomp drove him to reflect on the gospels. He
entered the Jesuits in 1585 and studied at Rome,
where he volunteered to help the plague stricken and
died a martyr of charity. He was only twenty-three
years old when he died.

John Carroll

John Carroll (1735-1815) studied with the Jesuits in
Maryland and became a Jesuit in Belgium. In 1774,
after Clement XIV suppressed the Jesuits, Carroll
returned to Maryland as a priest. He joined
Benjamin Franklin's fruitless effort to encourage
Canada to join the American Revolution. Appointed
in 1790 the first American bishop, he was stationed
in Baltimore where he encouraged education for men
and women and helped found Georgetown University
in 1789. He presided over the first national synod
of bishops in 1791, which laid down rules for the
American church. During his years as bishop, the
number of American Catholics quadrupled.

Gerard Manley Hopkins

Gerard Manley Hopkins (1844-1889) was an Englishman who wrote several of the prayer-poems printed in this book. He was educated at Oxford where he converted to Catholicism. In 1866 he entered the Jesuits; finishing his training, he served as a parish priest at Liverpool and a teacher at Dublin. Late in life he began writing poems that broke new ground in the use of the English language. His poems were not published until 1918, almost thirty years after his death.

Saint Peter Canisius

Saint Peter Canisius (1521-1597) was born in the Netherlands but studied at Cologne, Germany. He entered the Jesuits in 1543 and spent most of his life in Germany and Switzerland, founding Jesuit colleges, teaching, preaching, and writing his famous series of catechisms. He has been called the Second Apostle of Germany because he did so much to prevent the spread of Lutheranism in Germany and Austria.

Saint Francis Borgia

Saint Francis Borgia (1510-1572) was born into a wealthy Spanish family. His father was the Duke of Gandia in Valencia, and his mother was also of royal lineage. He married a noble lady, and together they had eight sons. But his wife died suddenly in 1546, and Borgia entered the Jesuits in 1548. In 1565, Borgia was elected the third superior general of the Jesuits. During his generalate, he revised the Jesuit constitutions, encouraged a deeper sense of personal prayer among Jesuits, built the Church of the Gesu in Rome, opened new mission territories in India and in North and South America, and used his wealth to reorganize the Roman College, which eventually became the Gregorian University.

Saint Edmund Campion

Saint Edmund Campion (1540-1581) was an Englishman who was martyred for his faith in London by Elizabeth I's government. His studies at Oxford converted him to Catholicism. He joined the Jesuits in France because the Jesuits were not allowed to operate in England during the reign of Queen Elizabeth. After his studies, he taught at Prague for several years before returning secretly to England in 1580. After a period of saying Mass for Catholics, he was captured, tortured, and executed.

Saint Francis Xavier

Saint Francis Xavier (1506-1552) was Ignatius Loyola's roommate at the University of Paris and an outstanding athlete. Together with four fellow students, they formed the nucleus that grew into the Jesuit order. Xavier was the first and greatest Jesuit missionary, spreading the Catholic faith in India and Indonesia. He was the first missionary to Japan and died as he was trying to enter China.

Traditional Prayers

Our Father

Our Father, who art in heaven,
  hallowed be thy name;
  thy kingdom come;
  thy will be done, on earth,
  as it is in heaven.
Give us this day our daily bread;
  and forgive us our trespasses
as we forgive those who trespass against us;
and lead us not into temptation,
but deliver us from evil.

Hail Mary

Hail, Mary, full of grace,
  the Lord is with thee.
Blessed art thou among women,
and blessed is the fruit of thy womb, Jesus.
Holy Mary, Mother of God, pray for us sinners,
  now and at the hour of our death. *Amen.*

Glory be to the Father

Glory be to the Father, and to the Son,
  and to the Holy Spirit,
As it was in the beginning, is now, and ever shall be,
world without end. *Amen.*

Gloria

Glory to God in the highest,
  and peace to his people on earth.
Lord God, heavenly King,
almighty God and Father,
  we worship you, we give you thanks,
  We praise you for your glory.
Lord Jesus Christ, only Son of the Father,
Lord God, Lamb of God,
you take away the sin of the world:
  have mercy on us;
you are seated at the right hand of the Father:
  receive our prayer.
For you alone are the Holy One,
you alone are the Lord,
you alone are the Most High,
  Jesus Christ,
  with the Holy Spirit,
  in the glory of God the Father. *Amen.*

Nicene Creed

We believe in one God,
the Father, the Almighty,
maker of heaven and earth,
of all that is seen and unseen.

We believe in one Lord, Jesus Christ,
the only Son of God,
eternally begotten of the Father,
God from God, Light from Light,
true God from true God,
begotten, not made, one in being with the Father.
Through him all things were made.
For us men and for our salvation
he came down from heaven:

by the power of the Holy Spirit
he was born of the Virgin Mary, and became man.

For our sake he was crucified under Pontius Pilate;
he suffered, died, and was buried.
On the third day he rose again
in fulfillment of the Scriptures;
he ascended into heaven
and is seated at the right hand of the Father.
He will come again in glory
to judge the living and the dead,
and his kingdom will have no end.

We believe in the Holy Spirit, the Lord,
   the giver of life,
   who proceeds from the Father and the Son.
   With the Father and the Son he is
     worshiped and glorified.
   He has spoken through the prophets.
   We believe in one, holy, catholic,
   and apostolic Church.
   We acknowledge one baptism
   for the forgiveness of sins.
   We look for the resurrection of the dead,
   and the life of the world to come. *Amen.*

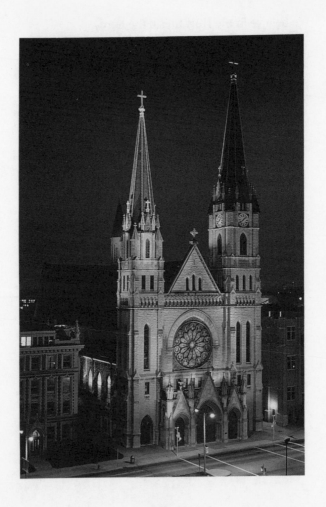

Apostles' Creed

I believe in God, the Father almighty,
   Creator of heaven and earth.
and in Jesus Christ, his only Son, our Lord.
He was conceived by the power of the Holy Spirit
   and born of the Virgin Mary.
He suffered under Pontius Pilate,
   was crucified, died, and was buried.
He descended to the dead.
On the third day he rose again.
He ascended into heaven,
   and is seated at the right
   hand of the Father.
He will come again
   to judge the living and the dead.
I believe in the Holy Spirit,
   the holy Catholic Church,
   the Communion of Saints,
   the forgiveness of sins,
   the resurrection of the body,
   and life everlasting. *Amen.*

Hail, Holy Queen

Hail, holy Queen, mother of mercy,
    our life, our sweetness, and our hope.
To you do we cry,
    poor banished children of Eve.
To you do we send up our sighs,
    mourning and weeping in this vale of tears.
Turn then, most gracious advocate,
    your eyes of mercy toward us,
    and after this exile
    show to us the blessed fruit of your
    womb, Jesus.
O clement, O loving,
O sweet Virgin Mary.
Pray for us, O Holy Mother of God.
That we may be made worthy of the promises of
Christ.

The Memorare

Remember, O most gracious Virgin Mary,
   that never was it known
   that anyone who fled to your protection,
   implored your help, or sought your
   intercession was left unaided.
Inspired by this confidence,
   we fly unto you,
O Virgin of virgins, our Mother!
To you we come, before you we stand,
   sinful and sorrowful.
O Mother of the Word incarnate,
   despise not our petitions,
   but in your mercy hear and answer us.
   Amen.

The Rosary

At its most basic, the rosary consists of five decades of Hail Marys (a decade means a group of ten), with each decade preceded by one Lord's Prayer and followed by one Glory Be to the Father. One chooses to recite the Joyful, Sorrowful, or Glorious mysteries (listed below), and before each decade, one states the mystery to be used for prayerful reflection. Even before starting the decades, however, one says a few preliminary prayers, corresponding to the crucifix and four beads.

How does one use all those beads? Suppose one were to pray the Joyful Mysteries, which are listed on page 53. One would proceed in the following way. As you recite each of the prayers listed below, move your fingers forward to the next bead or gap in the rosary.

Preliminary Prayers:
Crucifix: *The Apostles' Creed*
Separate Bead: *Our Father*
3 Beads: *3 Hail Marys*
Separate Bead: *Glory Be To the Father*

For the First Decade:

Gap:	*The Annunciation of the Angel Gabriel to Mary*
Separate Bead:	*Our Father*
10 Beads:	*10 Hail Marys*
Gap:	*Glory Be To the Father*

This sequence is repeated for each of the following four decades. The only change is the mystery that one proclaims at the beginning of the rosary. For example, the third Joyful Mystery is The Birth of Jesus in Bethlehem of Judea. After one completes the final Glory Be To the Father of the fifth mystery (The Finding of Christ in the Temple), one recites the Hail, Holy Queen, which completes the rosary.

To facilitate praying the rosary, all the prayers needed for the rosary are grouped together below.

The Rosary

Apostles' Creed

I believe in God, the Father almighty,
  Creator of heaven and earth.
I believe in Jesus Christ, his only Son, our Lord.
He was conceived by the power of the Holy Spirit
  and born of the Virgin Mary.
He suffered under Pontius Pilate,
  was crucified, died, and was buried.
He descended to the dead.
On the third day he rose again.
He ascended into heaven,
  and is seated at the right
  hand of the Father.
He will come again
  to judge the living and the dead.
I believe in the Holy Spirit,
  the holy Catholic Church,
  the Communion of Saints,
  the forgiveness of sins,
  the resurrection of the body,
  and life everlasting. *Amen.*

Our Father

Our Father, who art in heaven,
hallowed be thy name;
thy kingdom come;
thy will be done, on earth,
as it is in heaven.
Give us this day our daily bread;
and forgive us our trespasses
as we forgive those who trespass against us;
and lead us not into temptation,
but deliver us from evil. *Amen.*

Hail Mary

Hail, Mary, full of grace,
the Lord is with you.
Blessed are you among women,
and blessed is the fruit of your womb, Jesus.
Holy Mary, Mother of God, pray for us sinners,
now and at the hour of our death. *Amen.*

The Rosary

Glory Be to the Father

Glory be to the Father, and to the Son,
  and to the Holy Spirit,
As it was in the beginning, is now, and ever shall be,
  world without end. *Amen.*

Hail, Holy Queen

Hail, holy Queen, mother of mercy,
  our life, our sweetness, and our hope.
To you do we cry,
  poor banished children of Eve.
To you do we send up our sighs,
  mourning and weeping in this vale of tears.
Turn then, most gracious advocate,
  your eyes of mercy toward us,
  and after this exile
  show to us the blessed fruit of your
  womb, Jesus.
O clement, O loving, O sweet Virgin Mary.
Pray for us, O holy Mother of God.
That we may be made worthy of the promises of Christ.

The Rosary

The Joyful Mysteries
1. The Annunciation
   of the Angel Gabriel to Mary
2. The Visitation of Mary to Elizabeth
3. The Birth of Jesus
   in Bethlehem of Judea
4. The Presentation of Jesus
   in the Temple
5. The Finding of Jesus in the Temple

The Sorrowful Mysteries
1. The Agony of Jesus
   in the Garden of Gethsemane
2. The Scourging of Jesus at the Pillar
3. The Crowning of Jesus with Thorns
4. The Carrrying of the Cross
5. The Crucifixion and Death of Jesus

The Glorious Mysteries
1. The Resurrection of Jesus
2. The Ascension of Jesus into
   Heaven
3. The Descent of the Holy Spirit
   at Pentecost
4. The Assumption of Mary into
   Heaven
5. The Coronation of Our Lady

Angelus

Traditionally, the Angelus is recited at 6 a.m., noon, and again at 6 p.m. The person recites a short verse (V), then a response (R), followed by a Hail Mary. This pattern is repeated an additional three times and then a concluding prayer is recited.

V. The angel of the Lord declared unto Mary.
R. And she conceived of the Holy Spirit.
   Hail Mary, full of grace, etc.

V. Behold the handmaid of the Lord.
R. Be it done unto me according to your Word.
   Hail Mary, full of grace, etc.

V. And the Word was made flesh.
R. And dwelt among us.
   Hail Mary, full of grace, etc.

V. Pray for us, O holy Mother of God.
R. That we may be made worthy of the promises of Christ.

Pour forth, we beseech you, O Lord, Your grace into our hearts, that we, to whom the Incarnation of Christ, Your Son, was made known by the message of an angel, may, by His Passion and Cross, be brought to the glory of His Resurrection. Through Christ our Lord. *Amen.*

An Act of Contrition

O my God, I am heartily sorry for having offended Thee. I detest all my sins, because I dread the loss of Heaven and the pains of Hell, but most of all because I have offended Thee my God, who are all good and worthy of all my love. I firmly resolve, with the help of Thy grace, to confess my sins, to do penance, and to amend my life. *Amen.*

Soul of Christ

Soul of Christ, sanctify me.
Body of Christ, save me.
Blood of Christ, inebriate me.
Water from the side of Christ, wash me.
Passion of Christ, strengthen me.
O Good Jesus, hear me.
Within your wounds hide me.
Permit me not to be separated from you.
From the wicked foe, defend me.
At the hour of death, call me
and bid me come to you
That with your saints I may praise you
For ever and ever. *Amen.*

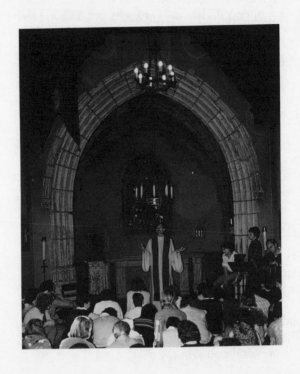

Canticle of Simeon
(Luke 1:68-79)

Blessed be the Lord, the God of Israel;
he has come to his people and set them free.

He has raised up for us a mighty savior,
born of the house of his servant David.

Through his holy prophets he promised of old
that he would save us from our enemies,
   from the hands of all who hate us.

He promised to show mercy to our fathers
and to remember his holy covenant.

This was the oath he swore to our father Abraham:
to set us free from the hands of our enemies,
   free to worship him without fear, holy
   and righteous in his sight
   all the days of our life.

You, my child, shall be called the prophet of the
Most High; for you will go before the Lord to
prepare his way, to give his people knowledge of
salvation by forgiveness of their sins. In the tender
compassion of our God, the dawn from
on high shall break upon us, to shine on those who
dwell in darkness and the shadow of death, and to
guide our feet into the way of peace.

Act of Faith

O my God, I firmly believe that you are one god in three divine Persons, Father, Son, and Holy Spirit; I believe that your divine Son became man and died for our sins, and that he will come to judge the living and the dead. I believe these and all the truths which the Holy Catholic Church teaches, because you revealed them, who can neither deceive nor be deceived.

Act of Hope

O my God, relying on your infinite goodness and promises, I hope to obtain pardon of my sins, the help of your grace, and life everlasting, through the merits of Jesus Christ, my Lord and Redeemer.

Act of Love

O my God, I love you above all things, with my whole heart and soul, because you are all good and worthy of all my love. I love my neighbor as myself for the love of you. I forgive all who have injured me and I ask pardon of all whom I have injured.

Morning Offering

O Jesus, through the Immaculate Heart of Mary, I offer you all my prayers, works, joys, and sufferings of this day in union with the Holy Sacrifice of the Mass throughout the world.

I offer them for all the intentions of your Sacred Heart: the salvation of souls, reparation for sin, the reunion of all Christians.

I offer them for the intentions of our bishops, and of all Apostles of Prayer, and in particular for those recommended by our Holy Father this month. *Amen.*

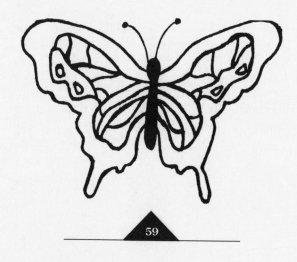

Magnificat
(Luke 1:46-55)

My soul magnifies the Lord, and my spirit rejoices
  in God my savior;
Because he has regarded the lowliness of His
  handmaid; for, behold, henceforth all generations
  shall call me blessed;
Because He who is mighty has done great things for
  me, and holy is His name;
And His mercy is from generation to generation on
  those who fear Him.

He has shown might with His arm, He has scattered
  the proud in the conceit of their heart.

He has put down the mighty from their thrones, and
  has exalted the lowly.

He has filled the hungry with good things, and the rich
  He has sent away empty.

He has given help to Israel,
His servant, mindful of his mercy—
  Even as He spoke to our fathers—to Abraham
  and to His posterity forever.

Daily Prayers

Prayer to My Guardian Angel

Angel of God, my guardian dear,
To whom God's love commits me here
Ever this day be at my side
To light and guard,
To rule and guide. *Amen.*

Night Prayer

Now I lay me down to sleep;
I pray the Lord my soul to keep.
If I should die before I wake,
I pray the Lord my soul to take. *Amen.*

Prayer for Marquette

God, Father and Mother of us all,
bless the goals of Marquette University,
and bestow your grace
on our strivings toward those goals.
Motivate all students to seek wisdom:
through conversing, writing, and criticizing;
through exploration and imagination.
Inspire our faculty with effective ways
to touch the minds of the young,
and with insights into the beauty of your universe.
Help our administrators and staff
to foster learning, research, and faith.
Watch over our alumni and friends;
encourage them to support Marquette generously.
Give success to our teams
and to our scholastic competitions;
grant us good health and good humor.
In our neighborhood and in our country,
help all people to live in safety
and to find productive jobs,
so that they can care for their families.
Most of all, help each of us
to grow in love and understanding
of your Son and our Brother, Jesus Christ, who is the
way to you, our Creator. *Amen.*

Grace Before Meals: Traditional

Bless us, O Lord, and these your gifts
which we are about to receive from your bounty.
Through Christ our Lord. *Amen.*

Grace Before Meals: The Whole Day

Lord Jesus be our holy guest,
Our morning prayer, our evening rest,
And with this daily food impart
Thy love and grace to every heart. *Amen.*

Grace Before Meals: German

Come, Lord Jesus, be our guest
and bless what thou hast given us. *Amen.*

Fellowship Grace
by Michael Buckley

Lord Jesus, who when you were on earth celebrated
a meal with joy, be with us now and fill us with
your spirit as we share food and fellowship together.
Amen.

A World Hunger Grace

For food in a world where many walk in hunger;
For faith in a world where many walk in fear,
For friends in a world where many walk alone,
We give you humble thanks, O Lord. *Amen.*

Prayer for Marquette Parents

Lord, bless my parents and watch over them. Keep them healthy and safe from all harm, and give them the strength to love and support one another. They have given me so much. Unfortunately, I occasionally forget their great love for me. Sometimes I become frustrated because I think they do not see the growth and maturity I have experienced. But I know they love me, and I love them dearly. Help me to show a mature love and respect for them. Bless them especially for all the sacrifices they make so that I can study and live at Marquette. Help me to become the son or daughter of which they can be proud, even if it is not quite the vision they have for me. *Amen.*

Prayer for Brothers and Sisters of a Marquette Student

Lord, sometimes I think you made brothers and sisters so that everyone has someone with whom they can disagree. As younger children, we had many arguments and fights, but we also had the most fun together. As I mature, give me insight so that I also appreciate the changes taking place in my brothers and sisters. I love them dearly. Give me the wisdom to express my love and concern wisely—in words to them, in deeds, and in prayer. Please give my younger siblings the desire and ability to attend Marquette. And bless my older siblings–who, among other things, are supposed to be praying for me. *Amen.*

Prayer for Jesuit Vocations

God our Father, You touched the heart of Your Son and called Him to His redeeming work. Through the illumination and inspiration of Your Holy Spirit, open the hearts of devout Catholic young men everywhere to a vocation to the Society of Jesus, and give them the grace to persevere in it, faithful to their vows and the spirit of Saint Ignatius Loyola. I ask that you strengthen me also in the same Ignatian spirit. *Amen.*

General Prayer for Vocations to Religious Life

Loving God, you will that all be saved and come to know the truth. Send forth laborers into the harvest so that all may hear your word of salvation, come to know your goodness, and respond to your love. Call generous women and men to follow you in simplicity of life, chastity, and obedience. May their special commitment be a constant support to your entire Church. *Amen.*

Irish Blessing I

May the road rise to meet you,
May the wind be at your back,
May the sun shine warm upon your face,
May the rains fall soft upon your field,
May God hold you in the palm of his hand.

An Old Irish Greeting

These things I warmly wish for you—
   Someone to love,
   Some work to do,
   A bit o' sun
   A bit o' cheer
   And a guardian angel
   Always near.

Irish Blessing II

With the first light of sun—
   Bless you.
When the long day is done—
   Bless you.
In your smiles and your tears—
   Bless you.
Through each day of your years—
   Bless you.

God, My Vision and Power
Irish (8th century, slightly updated)

Be thou my vision, O Lord of my heart,
Be all else but naught to me, save that thou art;
Be thou my best thought
   in the day and the night,
Both waking and sleeping, thy presence my light.
Be thou my wisdom, be thou my true word,
Be thou ever with me, and I with thee, Lord;
Be thou my great Father, and I thy true child;
Be thou my fine Mother, and I thy bright maid;
Be thou in my dwelling, and I with thee one.
Be thou my breastplate, my sword for the fight;
Be thou my whole armour,
   be thou my true might;
Be thou my soul's shelter,
   be thou my strong tower;
O raise thou me heavenward,
   great power of my power.
Riches I heed not, nor false and empty praise;
Be thou mine inheritance now and always;
Be thou and thou only the first in my heart:
O sovereign of heaven, my treasure thou art.
High king of heaven, thou heaven's bright sun.
O grant me its joys after vict'ry is won;
Great heart of my own heart, whatever befall,
Still be thou my vision, O ruler of all.

Various Prayers

Service of the Poor
by Mother Theresa of Calcutta

Make us worthy, Lord, to serve others throughout the world who live and die in poverty and hunger. Give them through our hands this day their daily bread, and by our understanding love, give peace and joy. *Amen.*

Prayer for My Friends at Marquette

Lord, keep my friends safe, caring, and funny. I enjoy being with them so much, just as you liked being with your friends, the Apostles. Sometimes my friends do things that hurt me, or they do damage to themselves or others. Forgive them, please, and keep them safe and healthy. Help me to contribute more to the vitality of my special group of friends. Make all of us true followers of Christ, but keep us lively and interesting. One day, make us all good parents, faithful and giving. *Amen.*

The Beatitudes

Blessed are the poor in spirit,
 for theirs is the kingdom of heaven.

Blessed are the meek,
 for they shall possess the earth.

Blessed are they who mourn,
 for they shall be comforted.

Blessed are they who hunger and thirst for justice,
 for they shall be satisfied.

Blessed are the merciful,
 for they shall obtain mercy.

Blessed are the clean of heart,
 for they shall see God.

Blessed are the peacemakers,
 for they shall be called children of God.

Blessed are they who suffer persecution for justice's sake,
 for theirs is the kingdom of heaven.

Blessed are you when men reproach you, and persecute
 you, and speak falsely,
 say all manner of evil against you, for My sake.

Prayer for the Pope

Lord, you have given the Pope awesome
responsibility as leader of Your Church. When I
think what I would do in His position, I think only
of myself, my friends, and the people I know. But
he has to consider all people and ethnic groups, from
many different cultures around the globe. It is too
much for any person to do on his own, and the Pope
knows he can only be effective with Your help. I
want to part of the solution, not the problem.
Sometimes, I disagree with the Pope. Despite these
differences, I respect him and I realize that you,
Lord, want us to support him. I pray that he listens
to You closely, and I also pray that You listen to me
before you speak to him. *Amen.*

Prayer for Racial Harmony

Dear Lord, it is clearly difficult for one race to interact well with another race, especially when there is a perceptible difference in skin color or physical features. I know how upset I become when I think someone is taking me for granted or using me. Lord, teach me to accept each person You send into my life as a messenger with important news. Help me to listen carefully to him or her and to admire the care with which You fashion each of Your messengers. They come in different shapes and hues, and the language may not be the same as mine. But I am grateful that You send them to me. *Amen.*

Prayer for Studying

Lord, I cannot believe how much time I waste. Please help me be more intense about my studies. I really am interested in things that the professor says in class. But when I finally sit down to study, I welcome distractions from studying so easily. You have given me a good mind, and you want me to explore your creation. Give me enthusiasm, Lord, for the subjects I am studying. Keep my eyes open and my mind on topic. Help me learn the material so that I can explain it clearly and convincingly to others, especially my friends. Jesus, you must have spent a lot of time reflecting on life to think of the wonderful parables that are recorded in the Gospels. Make me a good, critical thinker and help me to express myself clearly. Help me to use my mind for your greater Glory. *Amen.*

Prayer for Exams

God our Father, as I begin this time of exams,
I feel some anxiety and frustration. Help me to stay
focused. Give me a clear mind, to perform to the best
of my ability. Help me to study with dedication and
vigor. Grant me silence so that I may process the
knowledge I have obtained. Let me sleep peacefully at
night, so that I am refreshed and renewed for my
upcoming exams.

Be with me, Lord, during this time. Undoubtedly,
there will be moments when I want to quit and give up.
Please sustain me, Lord. Guide me during times of
trouble. Help me to realize that I have done my best
possible work. Let me be satisfied with the work I have
done, but also help me to see areas that I may improve
upon academically in the future. *Amen.*

Footprints
Anonymous

One night a man had a dream. He dreamed he was walking along the beach with the Lord. Across the sky flashed scenes from his life. For each scene, one belonged to him, and the other to the Lord.

When the last scene of his life flashed before him, he looked back at the footprints in the sand. He noticed that many times along the path of his life there was only one set of footprints. He also noticed that it happened at the very lowest and saddest times in his life.

This really bothered him and he questioned the Lord about it. "Lord, you said that once I decided to follow you, you'd walk with me all the way. But I have noticed that during the most troublesome times in my life, there is only one set of footprints. I don't understand why when I needed you most you would leave me."

The Lord replied, "My precious, precious child, I love you and I would never leave you. During your times of trial and suffering, when you only see one set of footprints, it was then that I carried you."

Consumer's Prayer
by Joyce M. Shutt

throwaway bottles
throwaway cans
throwaway friendships
throwaway fans

disposable diapers
disposable plates
disposable people
disposable wastes

instant puddings
instance rice
instance intimacy
instant ice

plastic dishes
plastic laces
plastic flowers
plastic faces

Lord of the living,
transcending our lives,
infuse us with meaning.
Recycle our lives.

Prayer for Vitality
by Rabindranath Tagore
(1861-1941)

When the heart is hard and parched up,
come upon me with a shower of mercy.
When grace is lost from life,
come with a burst of song.
When tumultuous work raises its din on all sides
shutting me out from beyond,
come to me, my Lord of silence,
with thy peace and rest.
When my beggarly heart sits crouched,
shut up in a corner,
break open the door, my king, and
come with the ceremony of a king.
When desire blinds the mind
with delusion and dust,
O thou holy one, thou wakeful one,
come with thy light and thy thunder.

Prayer for Purity
from the Book of Common Prayer

Almighty God, unto whom all hearts be open, all desires known, and from whom no secrets are hid; cleanse the thoughts of our hearts by the inspiration of thy Holy Spirit, that we may perfectly love thee and worthily magnify thy holy name; through Christ our Lord. *Amen.*

Prayer for Gratitude

You've blessed me with friends
and laughter and fun-
With rain that's as soft
as the light from the sun-
You've blessed me with stars
to brighten each night
You've given me help
to know wrong from right-
You've given me so much
Please, Lord give me too,
A heart that is always
Grateful to you.

Christ, My Beloved
by William Baldwin

Christ, my Beloved which still doth feed
  Among the flowers, having delight
  Among his faithful lilies,
Doth take great care for me indeed,
  And I again with all my might
  Will do what so his will is.

My Love in me and I in him,
  Conjoined by love, will still abide
  Among the faithful lilies
Till day do break, and truth do dim
  All shadows dark and cause them slide,
  According as his will is.

Prayer for Cheerfulness
by Robert Louis Stevenson
(1850-1894)

The day returns and brings us the petty round of
irritating concerns and duties. Help us to play the
man, help us to perform them with laughter and kind
faces, let cheerfulness abound with industry. Give us
to go blithely on our business this day, bring us to
our resting beds weary and content and undis-
honoured, and grant us in the end the gift of peace.

Prayer for Protection
by Saint Edmund of Abingdon
(c. 1175-1240)

Into thy hands, O Lord and father, we commend our souls and our bodies, our parents and our homes, friends and servants, neighbors and kindred, our benefactors and brethren departed, all thy people faithfully believing, and all who need thy pity and protection. Enlighten us with thy holy grace, and suffer us never more to be separated from thee, who art one God in Trinity, God everlasting. *Amen.*

Prayer for Enthusiasm
by John Henry Newman
(1801-1890)

Give me grace, O my Father, to be utterly ashamed of my own reluctance. Rouse me from sloth and coldness, and make me desire thee with my whole heart. Teach me to love meditation, sacred reading, and prayer. Teach me to love that which must engage my mind for all eternity. *Amen.*

In Coldness of Heart
by Saint Thomas More
(1478-1535)

O my sweet Saviour Christ, which in thine undeserved love towards mankind so kindly wouldst suffer the painful death of the cross, suffer me not to be cold nor lukewarm in love again towards thee.

Prayer for Serenity
by Reinhold Niebuhr

God, grant me the serenity to accept the things I cannot change, the courage to change the things I can, and the wisdom to know the difference.

Evening Prayer
by John Henry Newman
(1801-1890)

O Lord, support us all the day long, until the shadows lengthen and the evening comes, and the busy world is hushed, and the fever of life is over, and our work is done. Then, Lord, in thy mercy grant us a safe lodging, and a holy rest, and peace at last, through Jesus Christ our Lord.

Prayer for Loyalty
by Robert Louis Stevenson
(1850-1894)

Give us courage, gaiety and the quiet mind. Spare to
us our friends, soften to us our enemies. Bless us, if
it may be, in all our innocent endeavors. If it may
not, give us the strength to encounter that which is to
come, that we be brave in peril, constant in
tribulation, temperate in wrath, and in all changes of
fortune and down to the gates of death, loyal and
loving one to another.

For a Sense of Humor
by A.G. Bullivant

Give us a sense of humor, Lord, and also things
to laugh about. Give us the grace to take a joke
against ourselves, and to see the funny side of the
things we do. Save us from annoyance, bad temper,
resentfulness against our friends. Help us to laugh
even in the face of trouble. Fill our minds with the
love of Jesus; for his name's sake.

Asking Prayer

I asked God for strength that I might achieve,
   I was made weak
   that I might learn humbly to obey...
I asked for health that I might do greater things,
   I was given infirmity
   that I might do better things...
I asked for riches that I might be happy,
I was given poverty that I might be wise...
I asked for power
   that I might have the praise of persons,
I was given weakness
   that I might feel the need of God...
I asked for all things that I might enjoy life,
I was given life that I might enjoy all things...
I got nothing that I asked for-
   but everything I had hoped for...
Almost despite myself,
   my unspoken prayers were answered,
I am among all people most richly blessed.

Prayer for Self Knowledge
by Abu Bekr (died 634),
father-in-law of Muhammad

I thank thee, Lord, for knowing me better than I
know myself, and for letting me know myself better
than others know me. Make me, I pray, better than
they suppose, and forgive me what they do not
know.

Prayer for Fellow-workers
by Reinhold Niebuhr

O God, who hast bound us together in this bundle of
life, give us grace to understand how our lives
depend on the courage, the industry, the honesty, and
integrity of our fellow workers; that we may be
mindful of their needs, grateful for their faithfulness,
and faithful in our responsibilities to them, through
Jesus Christ our Lord. *Amen.*

The Difference

I got up early one morning
and rushed right into the day;
I had so much to accomplish
that I didn't have time to pray.
Problems just tumbled about me,
and heavier came each task.
"Why didn't God help me?" I wondered.
He answered, "You didn't ask."

I wanted to see joy and beauty,
but the day toiled on, grey and bleak;
I wondered why God didn't show me
He said, "But you didn't seek."
I tried to come into God's presence,
I used all my keys at the lock.
God gently and lovingly chided,
"My child, you didn't knock."

I woke up early this morning
and paused before entering the day;
I had so much to accomplish,
that I had to take time to pray.

The Clown's Prayer

"**A**s I tumble through this life help me to create
more laughter than tears,
dispense more happiness than gloom,
spread more cheer than despair,
Never let me become so indifferent
that I will fail to see
the wonder in the eyes of a child
or the twinkle in the eyes of the aged.
Never let me forget that my total effort
is to cheer people, make them happy and forget, at
least momentarily,
all the unpleasantness in their lives.
And in my final moment,
may I hear you whisper,
when you made my people smile,
you made me smile."

Divine Presence During the Day
Gelasian Sacramentary

Into Thy hands, O God, we commend ourselves, and
all who are dear to us, this day. Let the gift of Thy
special presence be with us even to its close. Grant
us never to lose sight of Thee all the day long, but to
worship, and pray to Thee, that at eventide we may
again give thanks unto Thee.

Thanksgiving in the Evening
by Robert Louis Stevenson
(1850-1894)

We come before thee, O Lord, in the end of thy day
with thanksgiving.
Our beloved in the far parts of earth, those who are
now beginning the labors of the day at the time at
which we end them, and those with whom the sun
now stands at the point of noon—bless, help,
console, and prosper them.
Our guard is relieved, the service of the day is over,
and the hour come to rest. We resign into thy hands
our sleeping bodies, our cold hearths and open doors.
Give us to awaken with smiles, give us to labor
smiling. As the sun returns in the east, so let our
patience be renewed with dawn. As the sun lightens
the world, so let our loving kindness make bright this
house of our habitation.

Compline

I will lay me down in peace and take my rest:
For it is thou Lord, only,
That makest me to dwell in safety.
Into thy hands, O Lord,
I commend my spirit,
For thou hast redeemed me,
O Lord, thou God of truth.

Prayer for Good Weather
by Hubert van Zeller, O.S.B.

Lord, Saint Benedict's sister prayed for rain and within an hour her prayer was heard. For the prophet Samuel and Elias thou didst do the same. Prayer, then, can get the weather changed, and this is something which nothing else can do. And so I ask for the purely temporary favor of fine weather, knowing that thy providence will decide upon, what, taken all in all, is best.

Prayer for the Homeless

Have mercy, O Lord our God, on those whom war or oppression or famine or a weak economy have robbed of homes and friends, and aid all those who try to help them. We commend also into your care those whose homes are broken by conflict and lack of love. Grant that where the love of women and men has failed, the divine compassion may heal. Grant my request through Jesus Christ our Lord.

Letter to a Young Activist
by *Thomas Merton*

Do not depend on the hope of results. When you are doing the sort of work you have taken on, you may have to face the fact that your work will be apparently worthless and even achieve no worth at all, if not perhaps, results opposite to what you expect. As you get used to this idea, you start more and more to concentrate not on the results, but in the value, the rightness, the truth of the work itself. And there, too, A great deal has to be gone through, as gradually you struggle less and less for an ideal, and more and more for specific people. The range tends to narrow down, and it gets more real. In the end, it is the reality of personal relationships that saves everything.

Love
by Thomas Cranmer
(1489-1556)

O Lord, who hast taught us that all our doings without love are nothing worth, send thy Holy Ghost, and pour into our hearts that most excellent gift of love, the very bond of peace and all virtues, without which whosoever liveth is counted dead before thee; grant us this for thy only Son Jesus Christ's sake.

Simple Riches

O God, who hast made the heaven and the earth and all that is good and lovely therein, and hast shown us through Jesus Christ our Lord that the secret of joy is a heart free from selfish desires, help us to find delight in simple things, and ever to rejoice in the riches of thy bounty, through Jesus Christ our Lord.

Opening-up: The Part of Love
by Saint Anselm
(1033-1109)

O Lord our God, grant us grace to desire thee with a whole heart, so that desiring thee we may seek and find thee; and so finding thee, may love thee; and loving thee, may hate those sins which separate us from thee, for the sake of Jesus Christ.

Purity, Like Nature
(O God the Holy Ghost)
by Christina Rossetti
(1830-1894)

O God the Holy Ghost
    who art Light unto thine elect,
    evermore enlighten us.
Thou who art Fire of Love,
    evermore enkindle us.
Thou who art Lord and Giver of Life,
    evermore replenish us.
As the wind is thy symbol,
    so forward our goings.
As the dove,
    so launch us heavenwards;
As water,
    so purify our spirits;
As a cloud,
    so abate our temptations;
As dew,
    so revive our languor;
As fire,
    so purge our dross.

The God Who Waits on Us
Leonine Sacramentary

Almighty and everlasting God, Who art
always more ready to hear than we to pray,
and art wont to give more than either
we desire or deserve, pour down upon
us the abundance of Thy mercy, forgiving
us those things whereof our conscience is
afraid, and giving us those things
which we are not worthy to ask.

Unite the Universe
Sarum Breviary

O God, who tellest the number of the stars,
and callest them all by names; heal,
we beseech Thee, the contrite in heart, and
gather together the outcasts, and enrich us
with the fullness of Thy wisdom.

Prayer for True Love

Lord, I am a child of the media. When I think of
love, images of movie and television stars come to
mind and words of popular songs dance in my brain.
Teach me about love that is more than romance, that
elevates me and my girlfriend or boyfriend to the
image in which You made us. Lord, teach us respect
for each other and your teachings. Help me to talk
to others about true love so that I do not deceive
myself.

The Holy Spirit

Come thou, Holy Spirit; restore the lives which,
without thee, are dead; kindle the hearts which,
without thee, are cold and dull; enlighten the minds
which, without thee, are dark and blind; fill the
Church which, without thee, is an empty shrine, and
teach us to pray.

Passing Prayer

Look graciously upon us, O Holy Spirit, and give us, for our hallowing, thoughts which pass into prayer, prayers which pass into love, and love which passes into life with thee for ever.

Refuge in God
by Saint Augustine
(354-430)

O Thou God, full of compassion, I commit and commend myself unto Thee, in whom I am, and live, and know. Be Thou the Goal of my pilgrimage, and my Rest by the way. Let my soul take refuge from the crowding turmoil of worldly thought beneath the shadow of Thy wings; let my heart, this sea of restless waves, find peace in Thee, O God.

A Cheerful Creature
by the Abbot of Grave

Lord, may I be wakeful at sunrise to begin a new day for thee, cheerful at sunset for having done my work for thee; thankful at moonrise and under starshine for the beauty of thy universe. And may I add what little may be in me to add to Thy great world.

Thanks for Life's Gifts
by Robert Louis Stevenson
(1850-1894)

We Thank Thee, Lord, for the glory of the late days and the excellent face of Thy sun. We thank Thee for good news received. We thank Thee for the pleasures we have enjoyed and for those we have been able to confer. And now, when the clouds gather and the rain impends, permit us not to be cast down; let us not lose the savor of past mercies and past pleasures; but, like the voice of a bird singing in the rain, let grateful memory survive in the hour of darkness. If there be in front of us any painful duty, strengthen us with the grace of courage; if any act of mercy, teach us tenderness and patience.

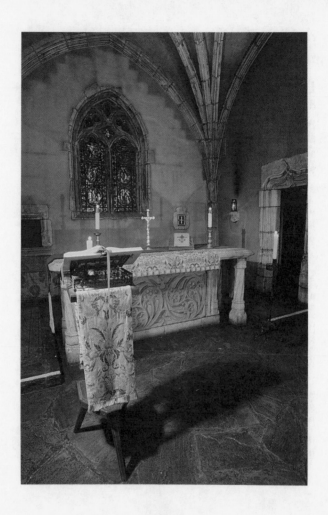

Prayer on the Door of Saint Stephen's Church, London

O God, make the door of this house
wide enough to receive all who need
human love and fellowship,
narrow enough to shut out
all envy, pride and strife.

Make its threshold smooth enough to be
no stumbling-block to children, nor to
straying feet, but rugged and strong
enough to turn back the tempter's power.

God make the door of this house
the gateway to Thine eternal kingdom.

Heavenly Rest
by John Donne
(1583-1631)

Bring us, O Lord God,
at our last awakening
into the house and gate of heaven,
to enter into that gate
and dwell in that house,
where there shall be
no darkness nor dazzling,
but one equal light;
no noise nor silence,
but one equal music;
no fears nor hopes,
but one equal possession;
no ends nor beginnings,
but one equal eternity;
in the habitations
of Thy glory and dominion
world without end. *Amen.*

Prayer of Generosity
by Saint Ignatius Loyola
(1491-1556)

Teach us, good Lord, to serve Thee
as Thou deservest;
to give and not to count the cost;
to fight and not to heed the wounds;
to toil and not to seek for rest;
to labor and not to ask for any reward,
save that of knowing that we do thy will.

Prayer for Penitence
by Christina Rossetti
(1830-1894)

O God, though our sins be seven,
though our sins be seventy times seven,
though our sins be more in number
than the hairs of our head,
yet give us grace in loving penitence
to cast ourselves down into the
depths of thy compassion.

Peace Prayer
by Saint Francis of Assisi
(1181-1226)

Lord, make me an instrument of thy peace:
Where there is hatred, let me sow love;
Where there is injury, pardon;
Where there is discord, union;
Where there is doubt, faith;
Where there is despair, hope;
Where there is darkness, light;
Where there is sadness, joy.

O Divine Master, grant that I may not so much seek
   To be consoled, as to console;
   To be understood, as to understand;
   To be loved, as to love;
For it is in giving that we receive,
It is in pardoning that we are pardoned,
And it is in dying that we are born
To Eternal Life.

Take and Receive
by Saint Ignatius Loyola
(1491-1556)

Take, Lord, and receive all my liberty, my memory, my understanding, and my entire will, all that I have and possess.

Thou hast given all to me. To Thee, O Lord, I return it. All is Thine, dispose of it wholly according to Thy will. Give me Thy love and Thy grace, for this is sufficient for me.

Prayer for Courage
by Robert Louis Stevenson
(1850-1894)

O God, grant me courage, gaiety of spirit and tranquillity of mind.

Learning Prayer
by George Herbert
(1593-1633)

Teach us, our God and king,
In all things thee to see,
That what we do in anything
We do it unto thee.

Light Amid Darkness
by George Dawson

O Lord our God, when the storm is loud, and the
night is dark, and the soul is sad, and the heart
oppressed: then, as weary travelers, may we look to
Thee; and beholding the light of Thy love, may it
bear us on, until we learn to sing Thy song in the
night.

For Receptivity
by Huub Oosterhuis

Make us receptive and open and may we accept your
kingdom like children taking bread from the hands of
their father. Let us live in your peace,
at home with you all the days of our lives.

Poems

The Windhover: To Christ our Lord
by Gerard Manley Hopkins, S.J.
(1844-1889)

I caught this morning morning's minion,
   kingdom of daylight's dauphin, dapple-dawn-
   drawn Falcon, in his riding
   Of the rolling level underneath him steady air,
   and striding
High there, how he rung upon the rein of a
   wimpling wing
In his ecstasy! then off, off forth on swing,
   As a skate's heel sweeps smooth on a bow-bend:
   the hurl and gliding
   Rebuffed the big wind. My heart in hiding
Stirred for a bird, —the achieve of,
   the mastery of the thing!

Brute beauty and valour and act,
   oh, air, pride, plume, here
Buckle! AND the fire that breaks from thee then,
   a billion
Times told lovelier, more dangerous, O my chevalier!

No wonder of it: sheer plod makes
   plough down sillion
Shine, and blue-bleak embers, ah my dear,
   Fall, gall themselves, and gash gold-vermilion.

Pied Beauty
by Gerard Manley Hopkins, S.J.
(1844-1889)

Glory be to God for dappled things—
For skies of couple-colour as a brindled cow;
For rose-moles
    all in stipple upon trout that swim;
Fresh-firecoal chestnut-falls; finches' wings;
Landscape plotted and pieced—
    fold, fallow, and plough;
And all trades, their gear and tackle and trim.
All things counter, original, spare, strange;
Whatever is fickle, freckled (who knows how?)
With swift, slow; sweet, sour; a dazzle, dim;
He fathers-forth whose beauty is past change:
    Praise him.

Spring and Fall: To a Young Child
by Gerard Manley Hopkins, S.J.
(1844-1889)

Margaret, are you grieving
Over goldengrove unleaving?
Leaves like the things of man, you
With your fresh thoughts care for, can you?
Ah! as the heart grows older
It will come to such sights colder
By and by, nor spare a sigh
Though worlds of wanwood leafmeal lie;
And yet you will weep and know why.
Now no matter, child, the name:
Sorrows springs are the same.
Nor mouth had, no nor mind, expressed
What heart heard of, ghost guessed:
It is the blight man was born for,
It is Margaret you mourn for.

Love

by George Herbert
(1593-1633)

Love bade me welcome; yet my soul drew back,
 Guilty of dust and sin.
But quick-ey'd Love, observing me grow slack
 From my first entrance in,
Drew nearer to me, sweetly questioning
 If I lack'd any thing.

'A guest', I answer'd, worthy to be here.'
 Love said, 'You shall be he.'
'I the unkind, ungrateful? Ah my dear,
 I cannot look on thee.'
Love took my hand, and smiling did reply,
 'Who made the eyes but I?'

'Truth Lord, But I have marr'd them;
 let my shame
Go where it doth deserve.'
'And know you not', says Love,
 'who bore the blame?'
 'My dear, then I will serve.'
'You must sit down', says Love,
 'and taste my meat.'
So I did sit and eat.

Moon-like is all other love
Anonymous
(14th Century)

Moon-like is all other love:
First crescent, then decreasing, gain;
Flower that buds, and soon goes off;
A day that fleets away in rain.

All other love bravely starts out,
But ends with torture, and in tears;
No love can salve the torment out
But that the King of Heaven bears:

For ever springing, ever new,
For ever the full orb, it is
A thing not thinned, from which accrue
Always new sweets, new centuries.

For this love, I all others fled:
Tell me where you may be found!
'Meek Mary is one fountainhead;
But Christ, Christ rather, is the ground.'

I did not find you, Christ found me.
Hold me, hold me fast, or else,
For all that love steadfast be,
This love of mine swerves as it swells.

And yet, and yet—I hurt, the blood
Floods from my heart. My God, I see,
Leaves me in this. So, well and good...
Yet still I pray: 'God be with me.'

Alas, what should I do in Rome?
I take a leaf from carnal love:
No mortal troth dare I trust home
Except He help that sits above.

The Holy Well

Anonymous
(16th Century)

As it fell out one May morning,
  And upon a bright holiday,
Sweet Jesus asked of his dear mother
  If he might go to play.
'To play, to play, sweet Jesus shall go,
  And to play now get you gone;
And let me hear of no complaint
  At night when you come home.'

Sweet Jesus went down to yonder town,
  As far as the Holy Well,
And there did see as fine children
  As any tongue can tell.
He said, 'God bless you every one,
  And your bodies Christ save and see!
And now, little children, I'll play with you,
  And you shall play with me.'

But they made answer to him, 'No!
  Thou art meaner than all of us;
Thou art but a simple fair maid's child,
  Born in an ox's stall.'
Sweet Jesus turned him round about,
  Neither laughed, nor smiled, nor spoke;
But the tears came trickling from his eyes
  Like waters from the rock.

Sweet Jesus turned him round about,
　To his mother's dear home went he,
And said, 'I have been in yonder town,
　As after you may see:
I have been down in yonder town,
　As far as the Holy Well;
There did I meet with as fine children
　As any tongue can tell.

'I said, "God Bless you every one,
　And your bodies Christ save and see!
And now, little children, I'll play with you,
　And you shall play with me."
But they made answer to me "No";
　They were lords' and ladies' sons,
And I the meanest of them all,
　Born in an ox's stall.'

'Though you are but a maiden's child,
　Born in an ox's stall,
Thou art the Christ, the King of Heaven,
　And the Savior of the m all!
Sweet Jesus, go down to yonder town,
　As far as the Holy Well,
And take away those sinful souls,
　And dip them deep in hell.'
'Nay, nay,' sweet Jesus smiled and said;
　'Nay, nay, that may not be,

For there are too many sinful souls
  Crying out for the help of me.'
Then up spoke the angel Gabriel,
  Upon a good set steven,
'Although you are but a maiden's child,
  You are the King of Heaven!'

Holy Sonnets V (Batter my heart)
by John Donne
(1572-1631)

Batter my heart, three-person'd God; for You
As yet but knock, breathe, shine, and seek to mend;
That I may rise and stand, o'erthrow me, and bend
Your force to break, blow, burn, and make me new.
I, like an usurp'd town, to another due
Labour to admit You, but O, to no end;
Reason, Your viceroy in me, me should defend,
But is captived, and proves weak or untrue.
Yet dearly I love you, and would be loved fain,
But am betrothed unto Your enemy;
Divorce me, untie, or break that knot again,
Take me to You, imprison me, for I
Except You enthral me, never shall be free,
Nor ever chaste, except You ravish me.

Peace
by Henry Vaughan
(1622-1695)

My soul, there is a country
 Far beyond the stars,
Where stands a winged sentry
 All skillful in the wars.
There, above noise and danger,
 Sweet peace sits crown'd with smiles,
And one born in a manger
 Commands the beauteous files.
He is thy gracious friend
 And (O my soul, awake!)
Did in pure love descend
 To die here for thy sake.
If thou canst get but thither,
 There grows the flower of peace,
The rose that cannot wither,
 Thy fortress, and thy ease.
Leave then thy foolish ranges;
 For none can thee secure
But one, who never changes,
 Thy God, thy life, thy cure.

The Lamb

by William Blake
(1757-1827)

Little Lamb, who made thee?
Dost thou know who made thee?
Gave thee life, & bid thee feed
By the stream & o'er the mead;
Gave thee clothing of delight,
Softest clothing, wooly, bright;
Gave thee such a tender voice,
Making all the vales rejoice?
Little Lamb, who made thee?
Dost thou know who made thee?

Little Lamb, I'll tell thee,
Little Lamb, I'll tell thee:
He is called by thy name,
For he calls himself a Lamb.
He is meek, & he is mild;
He became a little child.
I a child, & thou a lamb,
We are called by his name.
Little Lamb, God bless thee!
Little Lamb, God bless thee!

A Cradle Song
by William Blake
(1757-1827)

Sweet dreams, form a shade
O'er my lovely infant's head;
Sweet dreams of pleasant streams
By happy, silent, moony beams.

Sweet sleep, with soft down
Weave thy brows an infant crown.
Sweet sleep, Angel mild,
Hover o'er my happy child.

Sweet smiles, in the night
Hover over my delight;
Sweet smiles, Mother's smiles,
All the livelong night beguiles.

Sweet moans, dovelike sighs,
Chase not slumber from thy eyes.
Sweet moans, Sweeter smiles,
All the dovelike moans beguiles.

Sleep, sleep, happy child,
All creation slept and smil'd;
Sleep, sleep, happy sleep,
While o'er thee thy mother weep.

Sweet babe, in thy face
Holy image I can trace.
Sweet babe, once like thee,
Thy maker lay and wept for me,

Wept for me, for thee, for all,
When he was an infant small
Thou his image ever see,
Heavenly face that smiles on thee,

Smiles on thee, on me, on all;
Who became an infant small.
Infant smiles are his own smiles;
Heaven & earth to peace beguiles.

The Divine Image
by William Blake
(1757-1827)

To Mercy, Pity, Peace and Love
All pray in their distress;
And to these virtues of delight
Return their thankfulness.

For Mercy, Pity, Peace, and Love
Is God, our father dear,
And Mercy, Pity, Peace, and Love
Is Man, his child and care.

For Mercy has a human heart,
Pity a human face,
And Love, the human form divine,
And Peace, the human dress.

Then every man, of every clime,
That prays in his distress,
Prays to the human form divine,
Love, Mercy, Pity, Peace.

And all must love the human form,
In heathen, turk, or jew;
Where Mercy, Love, & Pity dwell
There God is dwelling too.

Holy Thursday
by William Blake
(1757-1827)

'Twas on a Holy Thursday, their innocent faces
  clean,
The children walking two & two, in red & blue &
  green,
Grey-headed beadles walk'd before, with wands as
  white as snow,
Till into the high dome of Paul's they like
  Thames' waters flow.

O what a multitude they seem'd, these flowers of
  London town!
Seated in companies they sit with radiance all their
  own.
The hum of multitudes was there, but multitudes of
  lambs,
Thousands of little boys & girls raising their
  innocent hands.

Now like a mighty wind they raise to heaven the
  voice of song,
Or like harmonious thunderings the seats of
  Heaven among.
Beneath them sit the aged men, wise guardians of
  the poor;
Then cherish pity, lest you drive an angel from
  your door.

The Tyger
by William Blake
(1757-1827)

Tyger! Tyger! burning bright
In the forests of the night,
What immortal hand or eye
Could frame thy fearful symmetry?

In what distant deeps or skies
Burnt the fire of thine eyes?
On what wings dare he aspire?
What the hand dare sieze the fire?

And what shoulder, & what art,
Could twist the sinews of thy heart?
And when thy heart began to beat,
What dread hand? & what dread feet?

What the hammer? what the chain?
In what furnace was thy brain?
What the anvil? what dread grasp
Dare its deadly terrors clasp?

When the stars threw down their spears,
And water'd heaven with their tears,
Did he smile his work to see?
Did he who made the Lamb make thee?

Tyger! Tyger! burning bright
In the forests of the night,
What immortal hand or eye,
Dare frame thy fearful symmetry?

The Eternal Goodness
by John Greenleaf Whittier
(1807-1892)

I know not what the future hath
  Of marvel or surprise,
Assured alone that life and death
  His mercy underlies.
And if my heart and flesh are weak
  To bear an untried pain,
The bruised reed he will not break,
  But strengthen and sustain.
No offering of my own I have,
  Nor works my faith to prove;
I can but give the gifts he gave,
  And plead his love for love.
And so beside the silent sea
  I wait the muffled oar;
No harm from him can come to me
  On ocean or on shore.

I know not where his islands lift
  Their fronded palms in air;
I only know I cannot drift
  Beyond his love and care.

Jerusalem
by William Blake
(1757-1827)

And did those feet in ancient time
Walk upon England's mountains green?
And was the holy Lamb Of God
On England's pleasant pastures seen?

And did the Countenance Divine
Shine fourth upon our clouded hills?
And was Jerusalem builded here
Among these dark Satanic Mills?

Bring me my Bow of Burning gold!
Bring me my Arrows of desire!
Bring me my spear! O clouds, unfold!
Bring me my Chariot of fire!

I will not cease from Mental Fight,
Nor shall my Sword sleep in my hand,
Till we have built Jerusalem
In England's green and pleasant land.

Walking with God

by William Cowper
(1731-1800)

Oh! for a closer walk with God,
 A calm and heavenly frame;
A light to shine upon the road
 That leads me to the Lamb!

Where is the blessedness I knew
 When first I saw the Lord?
Where is the soul-refreshing view
 Of Jesus and his word?

What peaceful hours I once enjoyed!
 How sweet their memory still!
But they have left an aching void
 The world can never fill.

Return, O holy Dove, return,
 Sweet messenger of rest;
I hate the sins that made thee mourn,
 And drove thee from my breast.

The dearest idol I have known,
 Whate'er that idol be,
Help me to tear it from thy throne,
 And worship only Thee.

So shall my walk be close with God,
  Calm and serene my frame;
So purer light shall mark the road
  That leads me to the Lamb.

Free Grace

by Charles Wesley
(1707-1798)

And can it be, that I should gain
  An interest in the Saviour's blood?
Died he for me, who caused his pain,
  For me, who him to death pursued?
Amazing Love! How can it be
That thou, my God, Shouldst die for me?

'Tis Mystery all! the Immortal dies!
  Who can explore his strange design?
In vain the first-born seraph tries
  To sound the depths of Love divine.
'Tis Mercy all! Let earth adore;
Let angel minds enquire no more.

He left his Father's throne above,
  (So free, so infinite his Grace!)
Emptied himself of all but Love,
  And bled for Adam's helpless race;
'Tis Mercy all, immense and free!
For, O my God, it found out me!

Long my imprisoned spirit lay,
 Fast bound in sin and nature's night.
Thine eye diffused a quickening ray;
 I woke; the dungeon flamed with light;
My chains fell off, my heart was free,
I rose, went forth, and followed thee.

Still the small inward voice I hear
 That whispers all my sins forgiven;
Still the atoning blood is near
 That quenched the wrath of hostile heaven.
I feel the life his wounds impart;
I feel my savior in my heart.

No condemnation now I dread.
 Jesus, and all in him, is mine;
Alive in him, my living Head,
 And clothed in Righteousness divine,
Bold I approach the eternal throne,
And claim the crown, through Christ, my own.

Lead, Kindly Light
by John Henry Newman
(1801-1890)

Lead, kindly light, amid the encircling gloom,
    Lead thou me on;
The night is dark, and I am far from home;
    Lead thou me on.
Keep thou my feet; I do not ask to see
The distant scene: one step enough for me.

I was not ever thus, nor prayed that thou
    Shouldst lead me on;
I loved to choose and see my path; but now
    Lead thou me on.
I loved the garish day, and, spite of fears,
Pride ruled my will: remember not past years.

So long thy power hath blest me, sure it still
    Will lead me on
O'er moor and fen, o'er crag and torrent, till
    The night is gone,
And with the morn those angels faces smile
Which I have loved long since, and lost awhile.

You, Neighbor God
by Rainer Maria Rilke
(1875-1926)

You, neighbor God, if sometimes in the night
I rouse you with loud knocking, I do so
only because I seldom hear you breathe;
And I know: you are alone.
And should you need a drink, no one is there
to reach it to you, groping in the dark.
Always I harken. Give but a small sign.
I am quite near.

Between us there is but a narrow wall,
and by sheer chance; for it would take
merely a call from your lips or from mine
to break it down,
and that without a sound.

The wall is builded of your images.
They stand before you hiding you like names.
And when the light with me blazes high
that in my inmost soul I know you by,
the radiance is squandered on their frames.

And then my senses, which too soon grow lame,
exiled from you, must go their homeless ways.

from *The Dream of Gerontius*
by John Henry Newman
(1801-1890)

Praise to the holiest in the height,
And in the depth be praise,
In all his words most wonderful,
Most sure in all his ways.

Oh loving wisdom of our God!
When all was sin and shame,
A second Adam to the fight
And to the rescue came.

Oh wisest love! that flesh and blood,
Which did in Adam fail,
Should strive afresh against the foe,
Should strive and should prevail;

And that a higher gift than grace
Should flesh and blood refine,
God's presence and his very self,
And essence all-divine.

Oh generous love! that he who smote
In man for man the foe,
The double agony in man
For man should undergo,

And in the garden secretly,
And on the cross on high,
Should teach his brethren, and inspire
To suffer and to die.

Praise to the holiest in the height,
And in the depth be praise,
In all his words most wonderful,
Most sure in all his ways.

Precious Gift
by Gladys Adkins

Today is mine, it belongs to me,
To live the best I can.
To shape, to mold, for eternity
A day that is simply grand.

I mustn't fill it with petty things,
Selfish things, and small.
I must live only for the joy it brings
To give my best my all.

God made it such a beautiful day.
A special day, you see.
He made it bright and shining,
Then, He gave it to me.

You, too, are given a special day,
A day in which to give
The very best within you
Every day you live.

Psalms

Psalm 34

I will bless the Lord at all times,
his praise always on my lips;
in the Lord my soul shall make its boast.
The humble shall hear and be glad.

Glorify the Lord with me.
Together let us praise his name.
I sought the Lord and he answered me;
from all my terrors he set me free.

Look towards him and be radiant;
let your faces not be abashed.
This poor man called; the Lord heard him
and rescued him from all his distress.

The angel of the Lord is encamped
around those who revere him, to rescue them.
Taste and see that the Lord is good.
He is happy who seeks refuge in him.

Revere the Lord, you his saints.
They lack nothing, those who revere him.
Strong lions suffer want and go hungry
but those who seek the Lord lack no blessing.

Psalm 42: Longing for the Lord

Like the deer that yearns
for running streams,
so my soul is yearning
for you, my God.

My soul is thirsting for God,
the God of my life;
when can I enter and see
the face of God?

My tears have become my bread,
by night, by day,
as I hear it said all the day long:
"Where is your God?"

These things will I remember
as I pour out my soul:
how I would lead the rejoicing crowd
into the house of God,
amid cries of gladness and thanksgiving,
the throng wild with joy.

My soul is cast down, my soul,
why groan within me?
Hope in God; I will praise him still,
my savior and my God.

My soul is cast down within me
as I think of you,
from the country Jordan and Mount Hermon,
from the Hill of Mizar.

Deep is calling on deep,
in the roar of waters:
your torrents and all your waves
swept over me.

By day the Lord will send
his loving kindness;
by night I will sing to him,
praise the God of my life.

I will say to God, my rock:
"Why have you forgotten me?
Why do I go mourning,
oppressed by the foe?"

With cries that pierce me to the heart,
my enemies revile me,
saying to me all the day long:
"Where is your God?"

Why are you cast down, my soul,
why groan within me?
Hope in God; I will praise him still,
my savior and my God.

Psalm 104

Bless the Lord, my soul!
Lord God, how great you are,
clothed in majesty and glory,
wrapped in light as in a robe!

You stretch out the heavens like a tent.
Above the rains you build your dwelling.
You make the clouds your chariot,
and walk on the wings of the wind;
you make the winds your messengers
and flashing fire your servants.

You founded the earth on its base,
to stand firm from age to age.
You wrapped it with the ocean like a cloak:
the waters stood higher than the mountains.

At your threat they took to flight;
at the voice of your thunder they fled.
They rose over the mountains and flowed down
to the place which you had appointed.
You set limits they might not pass
lest they return to cover the earth.

You make springs gush forth in the valleys:
they flow in between the hills.
They give drink to all the beasts of the field;
the wild-asses quench their thirst.
On their banks dwell the birds of heaven;
from the branches they sing their song.

From your dwelling you water the hills;
earth drinks its fill of your gift.
You make the grass grow for the cattle
and the plants to serve man's needs,

that he may bring forth bread from the earth
and wine to cheer man's heart;
oil, to make him glad
and bread to strengthen man's heart.

The trees of the Lord drink their fill,
the cedars he planted on Lebanon;
there the birds build their nests:
on the tree-top the stork has her home.
The goats find a home on the mountains
and rabbits hide in the rocks.

You made the moon to mark the months;
the sun knows the time for its setting.
When you spread the darkness it is night
and all the beasts of the forest creep forth.
The young lions roar for their prey
and ask their food from God.

At the rising of the sun they steal away
and go to rest in their dens.
Man goes forth to his work,
to labor till evening falls.

Psalm 138

I will give thanks to you, O Lord, with all my heart,
　for you have heard the words of my mouth;
in the presence of the angels I will sing your praise;
I will worship at your holy temple
　and give thanks to your name,
Because of your kindness and your truth;
　for you have made great above all things
　your name and your promise.
When I called, you answered me;
　you built up strength within me.

All the kings of the earth shall give thanks to you, O Lord,
　when they hear the words of your mouth;
And they shall sing of the ways of the Lord:
　"Great is the glory of the Lord."
The Lord is exalted, yet the lowly he sees,
　and the proud he knows from afar.

Though I walk amid distress, you preserve me;
　against the anger of my enemies you raise your hand;
　your right hand saves me.
The Lord will complete what he has done for me;
　your kindness, O Lord, endures forever;
　forsake not the work of your hands.

Hymns

Morning Has Broken

Morning has broken
Like the first morning,
Blackbird has spoken
Like the first bird.
Praise for the singing!
Praise for the morning!
Praise for them, springing
Fresh from the Word!

Sweet the rains new fall
Sunlit from heaven,
Like the first dew fall
On the first grass.
Praise for the sweetness
Of the wet garden,
Sprung in completeness
Where his feet pass.

Mine is the sunlight!
Mine is the morning,
Born of the one light
Eden saw play!
Praise with elation,
Praise every morning,
God's re-creation
Of the new day!

Amazing Grace!

Amazing Grace! How sweet the sound
that saved a wretch like me!
I once was lost, but now am found,
Was blind, but now I see!

'Twas grace that taught my heart to fear,
And grace my fears relieved.
How precious did that grace appear,
The hour I first believed!

The Lord has promised good to me,
His Word my hope secures.
He will my shield and portion be
As long as life endures.

Through many dangers, toils and snares,
I have already come.
His grace has brought me safe thus far,
His grace will lead me home.

Yes, when this flesh and heart shall fail
And mortal life shall cease,
Amazing grace shall then prevail
In heaven's joy and peace.

On Eagle's Wings

You who dwell in the shelter of the Lord,
who abide in his shadow for life,
say to the Lord:
"My refuge, my rock in whom I trust!"

Refrain:
And he will raise you up on eagle's wings,
bear you on the breath of dawn,
make you to shine like the sun,
and hold you in the palm of his hand.
And hold you, hold you in the palm of his hand.

The snare of the fowler will never capture you,
and famine will bring you no fear;
under his wings your refuge,
his faithfulness your shield.

You need not fear the terror of the night,
nor the arrow that flies by day;
though thousands fall about you,
near you it shall not come.

For to his angels he's given a command
to guard you in all of your ways;
upon their hands they will bear you up,
lest you dash your foot against a stone.

How Great Thou Art

O Lord my God! When I in awesome wonder
Consider all the worlds thy hands have made,
I see the stars, I hear the rolling thunder,
Thy pow'r throughout the universe displayed;

Refrain:
Then sings my soul, my Saviour God to thee;
How great thou art, how great thou art!
Then sings my soul, my Saviour God to thee;
How great thou art, how great thou art!

When through the woods and forest glades
    I wander
And hear the birds sing sweetly in the trees;
When I look down from lofty mountain grandeur
And hear the brook and feel the gentle breeze;

And when I think that God, his Son not sparing,
Sent him to die, I scarce can take it in;
That on the cross my burden gladly bearing,
He bled and died to take away my sin;

When Christ shall come with shout of acclamation
And take me home, what joy shall fill my heart!
Then I shall bow in humble adoration
And there proclaim, my God, how great thou art!

All My Days

Refrain:
Till the end of my days, O Lord,
I will bless your name, sing your praise,
give you thanks, all my days.

You have made me little less than a god,
And have lavished my heart with Your love.
With dignity and honor you've clothed me,
given me rule over all.

You have blessed me with good things and plenty
And surrounded my table with friends.
Their love and their laughter enrich me;
together we sing your praise.

Your sun and your moon give me light,
And your stars show the way through the night.
Your rivers and streams have refreshed me.
I will sing your praise.

How great is your love, O Father,
That you sent us your savior son.
His death and His rising will heal us,
And draw us all unto You.

Be Not Afraid

You shall cross the barren desert,
But you shall not die of thirst.
You shall wander far in safety
Though you do not know the way.
You shall speak your words in foreign lands
And all will understand.
You shall see the face of God and live.

Refrain:
Be not afraid. I go before you always.
Come follow me, and I will give you rest.

If you pass through raging waters in the sea
You shall not drown.
If you walk amid the burning flames,
You shall not be harmed.
If you stand before the pow'r of hell
and death is at your side,
know that I am with you through it all.

Blessed are your poor,
for the kingdom shall be theirs.
Blest are you that weep and mourn,
for one day you shall laugh.
And if wicked men insult and hate you
all because of me,
blessed, blessed are you!

Come with Me into the Fields

The fields are high and summer's days are few;
green fields have turned to gold.
The time is here for the harvesting.
For gathering home into barns.

Refrain:
The harvest is plenty; laborers are few.
Come with me into the fields. Your
arms may grow weary; your shoes will wear thin.
Come with me into the fields.

The seeds were sown by other hands than yours;
nurtured and cared for they grew.
But those who have sown will not harvest them;
The reaping will not be their care.

Though the Mountains May Fall

Refrain:
Though the mountains may fall
and the hills turn to dust,
yet the love of the Lord will stand,
as a shelter for all who will call on his name.
Sing the praise and the glory of God.

Could the Lord ever leave you?
Could the Lord forget his love?
Though a mother forsake her child,
he will not abandon you.

Should you turn and forsake him,
he will gently call your name.
Should you wander away from him,
he will always take you back.

Go to him when you're weary;
he will give you eagle's wings.
You will run, never tire,
for your God will be your strength.

As he swore to your fathers,
when the flood destroyed the land.
He will never forsake you;
he will swear to you again.

Praise the Lord, My Soul

Praise the Lord, my soul,
let fire and rain give praise to him,
Give praise to him,
who is merciful, slow to judge;
bless the Lord, O my soul.

Bless the Lord, my soul,
let all I am give praise to him,
and not forget he is kind, he forgives our sins;
bless the Lord, O my soul.

Merciful and kind,
He knows our ways, he knows we're dust;
and like the flowers that flourish,
we soon must die;
bless the Lord, O my soul.

Glory to our God,
let all that is give praise to him;
give praise to him, all you creatures
  who live his love;
bless the Lord, O my soul,
bless the Lord, O my soul.

Earthen Vessels

Refrain:
We hold a treasure, not made of gold,
in earthen vessels, wealth untold,
one treasure only: the Lord, the Christ,
in earthen vessels.

Light has shown in our darkness:
God has shown in our heart,
with the light of the glory
of Jesus, the Lord.

He has chosen the lowly,
who are small in this world;
In his weakness is glory,
In Jesus, the Lord.

Glory and Praise to Our God

Refrain:
Glory and praise to our God, who
alone gives light to our days.
Many are the blessings he bears to
those who trust in his ways.

We, the daughters and sons of him
who built the valleys and plains,
praise the wonders our God has done
in ev'ry heart that sings.

In his wisdom he strengthens us
like gold that's tested in fire.
Though the power of sin prevails,
our God is there to save.

Ev'ry moment of ev'ry day
our God is waiting to save,
always ready to seek the lost,
to answer those who pray.

God has watered our barren land
and spent his merciful rain.
now the rivers of life run full
for anyone to drink.

I Lift Up My Soul

To you, Yahweh, I lift up my soul, O my God.
To you, Yahweh, I lift up my soul, O my God.

Yahweh, show your ways to me.
Teach me your paths
and keep me in the ways of your truth,
for you are the God that saves me.

The Lord is so good, so holy,
sinners find the way,
and in all that is right he guides the humble;
the poor he leads in his pathways.

All day long I hope in your goodness.
Remember your love,
the love that you promised long ago,
and the kindness that you gave from of old.

Only in God

Refrain:
Only in God will my soul be at rest.
From him comes my hope, my salvation.
He alone is my rock of safety,
my strength, my glory, my God.

Trust in him at all times, O people,
and pour out your hearts.
God himself is a refuge for us
and a stronghold for our fear.

Many times have I heard him tell
of his long lasting love.
You yourself, Lord, reward all who labor
for love of your name.

Take, Lord, Receive

Take, Lord, receive
all my liberty,
my memory, understanding,
my entire will.

Refrain:
Give me only your love and your grace:
that's enough for me.
Your love and your grace are enough for me.

Take, Lord, receive
all I have and possess.
You have given all to me;
now I return it.

Take, Lord, receive,
all is yours now;
dispose of it wholly
according to your will.

Yahweh, The Faithful One

Refrain:
Yahweh's love will last forever,
his faithfulness 'til the end of time.
Yahweh is a loving God,
Yahweh, the faithful One.

Have no fear, for I am with you;
I will be your shield.
Go now and leave your homeland,
for I will give you a home.

You shall be my chosen people,
and I will be your God.
I will bless your name forever
and keep you from all harm.

Look up and see the heavens
and count the stars if you can.
Your name will be even greater,
greater than all these stars.

See now the land before you,
rich with food and rain.
No longer must you wander,
for this will be your home.

Holy God, We Praise Thy Name

Holy God, we praise thy Name;
Lord of all, we bow before thee!
All on earth thy sceptre claim.
All in heaven above adore thee.
Infinite thy vast domain,
Everlasting is thy reign!

Holy Father, Holy Son,
Holy Spirit, three we name thee,
While in essence only One,
Undivided God we claim thee:
And adoring bend the knee,
While we own the mystery.

Sing a New Song

Refrain:
Sing a new song unto the Lord;
let your song be sung from mountains high.
Sing a new song unto the Lord,
    singing alleluia.

Yahweh's people dance for joy.
O come before the Lord.
And play for him on glad tambourines,
and let your trumpets sound

Rise, O children, from your sleep;
your savior now has come.
He has turned your sorrow to joy,
and filled your soul with song.

Glad my soul for I have seen
the glory of the Lord.
The trumpet sounds; the dead shall be raised.
I know my savior lives.

You Are Near

Refrain:
Yahweh, I know you are near,
standing always at my side.
You guard me from the foe,
and you lead me in ways everlasting.

Lord, you have searched my heart,
and you know when I sit and when I stand.
Your hand is upon me protecting me from death,
keeping me from harm.

Where can I run from your love?
If I climb to the heavens you are there;
if I fly to the sunrise or sail beyond the sea,
Still I'd find you there.

You know my heart and its ways,
you who formed me before I was born.
In the secret of darkness I saw the sun
in my mother's womb.

Marvelous to me are your works;
how profound are your thoughts, my Lord.
Even if I could count them,
they number as the stars,
you would still be there.

Acknowledgments

Marquette University gratefully acknowledges the following publishers for permission to include the indicated materials in this book. For purposes of identification, titles have been created in this book for some of the prayers. They are used as references in the acknowledgments below. The gratitude of the University is extended to:

Mayhew-McCrimmon (Southend-on-Sea, Great Britain) for the following prayers: "God, My Vision and Power" (Irish, 8th century), "Prayer for Courage," "Learning Prayer," "Prayer for Vitality," "Prayer for Purity," "Prayer for Cheerfulness," "Prayer for Protection," "Prayer for Enthusiasm," "Prayer for Serenity," "Evening Prayer," "Service of the Poor," "Prayer for Loyalty," "For a Sense of Humor," "Prayer for Good Weather," "Prayer for Self Knowledge," "Prayer for Fellow-workers," "Prayer for the Homeless," "Thanksgiving in the Evening," "Simple Riches," "Opening-up: The Part of Love," "For Receptivity," "Purity, Like Nature" (C. Rossetti), "Love," "Muslim Prayer," "The Holy Spirit," "Passing Prayer," all of which are taken from *The One Who Listens: A Book of Prayer* by Michael Hollings and Etta Gullick (1971).

Peter Pauper Press (Mount Vernon, New York) for "The God Who Waits on Us," "Unite the Universe," "Patience," "Prayer on the Door of Saint Stephen's Church, London," "Refuge in God," "A Cheerful Creature," "Thanks for Life's Gifts," "Light Amid Darkness," "Heavenly Rest," "Prayer for Generosity," "Prayer for Penitence," "Take and Receive," "Peace Prayer," "God, My Vision and Power," taken from *Little Book of Prayers* (1960).

Hodder and Stoughton (London) for "Grace Before Meals: Traditional," "Grace Before Meals: The Whole Day," "Grace Before Meals: German," "Fellowship Grace," and "World

Hunger Grace," taken from *The Treasury of the Holy Spirit,* written and complied by Msgr. Michael Buckley (1984).

Kilkenny Press (New York) for "Irish Blessing I," "An Old Irish Greeting," "Irish Blessing II," and "Prayer for Gratitude," taken from *Irish Blessings: An Illustrated Edition* (1990).

The Catholic Book Publishing Company (New York) for the Canticle of Simeon, Psalms 34, 42, and 104, and "Morning Has Broken," "Holy Sonnets V" (Batter my heart), "You, Neighbor God," "The Hound of Heaven," taken from *The Liturgy of the Hours* (1975).

Penguin Books (New York) for the poems "The Windhover," "Pied Beauty," and "Spring and Fall: To a Young Child," taken from *Poems and Prose of Gerard Manley Hopkins,* edited by W.H. Gardner (1953).

Springbook Publications (Fraser, Michigan) for "The Difference" (1986).

John Patrick Donnelly, S.J., for information about Saint Ignatius, the history of the Jesuits, Saint Joan of Arc, and brief sketches of individual Jesuits in this collection.

John J. Piderit, S.J., for "Prayer for Marquette," "Prayer for Marquette Parents," "Prayer for Brothers and Sisters of a Marquette Student," "Prayer for Jesuit Vocations," "Prayer for My Friends at Marquette," "Prayer for Studying,' "Prayer for the Pope," and "Prayer for Racial Harmony,"

Kathryn M. Oberhauser, A&S '91, for the drawings that grace these pages.

Casey Beaumier, CJPA '93, for "Prayer for Exams."

Michael J. Burns, A&S '65, for the life of Saint Francis Borgia, "The Church of the Gesu," and "Jacques Marquette."

Salesian Missions (New Rochelle, New York) for "Precious Gift," taken from *Life's Treasure* (1987).

Oxford University Press (New York) for "Jerusalem," "Christ, my Beloved," excerpts from "The Dream of Gerontius," 'Moon- like is all other love,' "The Holy Well," "Love," "Peace" (G. Herbert), "Peace" (H. Vaughan), "Free Grace," Walking with God," "The Eternal Goodness," "Lead, Kindly Light," taken from *The New Oxford Book of Christian Verse,* Donald Davie, editor (1981).

J.S. Paluch Company, Inc., for "Amazing Grace," "On Eagle's Wings," "America the Beautiful," "How Great Thy Art," and "Holy God, We Praise Thy Name."

The North American Liturgy Resources (Phoenix, Arizona) for "All My Days," "Be Not Afraid," "Come With Me Into the Fields," "Earthen Vessels," "Glory and Praise to Our God," "I Lift Up My Soul," "Only in God," "Praise the Lord, My Lord," "Sing a New Song," "Take, Lord, Receive," "Though the Mountains May Fall," "Yahweh, the Faithful One," and "You Are Near," taken from *Songs of the Saint Louis Jesuits* (1978).

"The Mennonite" for the Consumers' Prayer.

The Jesuits of Loyola University, Chicago, for "Prayer for Jesuit Vocations" and "General Prayer for Vocations to Religious Life."

The Sinsinawa Dominicans for "The Clown's Prayer," and "Asking Prayer."

Other contributors whose prayers have been passed on anonymously.